FIRST BUT FORGOTTEN

— THE UNTOLD STORY OF —
JACK JOHNSON
HEAVYWEIGHT BOXING LEGEND

BY ELLIOTT SMITH

CAPSTONE PRESS
a capstone imprint

Published by Capstone Press, an imprint of Capstone
1710 Roe Crest Drive, North Mankato, Minnesota 56003
capstonepub.com

Copyright © 2025 by Capstone. All rights reserved. No part of this publication may be reproduced in whole or in part, or stored in a retrieval system, or transmitted in any form or by any means, electronic, mechanical, photocopying, recording,
or otherwise, without written permission of the publisher.

Library of Congress Cataloging-in-Publication Data is available
on the Library of Congress website.

ISBN: 9781669070191 (hardcover)
ISBN: 9781669070146 (paperback)
ISBN: 9781669070153 (ebook PDF)

Summary: You may have heard about Muhammad Ali. But long before Ali entered the ring, Black boxer Jack Johnson was winning bouts and challenging ideas about race. Uncover Jack Johnson's story and how his life and career demonstrate the challenges of being Black, talented, and famous in the United States.

Editorial Credits
Editor: Ericka Smith; Designer: Sarah Bennett; Media Researcher: Svetlana Zhurkin; Production Specialist: Katy LaVigne

Image Credits
Alamy: Dom Slike, 29, Motoring Picture Library, 20; Associated Press: 28; Getty Images: Chicago History Museum/Chicago Daily News Collection/Chicago Sun-Times, 15, Hulton Archive, cover, 21 (right), The Ring Magazine, 13, ullstein bild/Philipp Kester, 17; Granger: 9; Library of Congress: 5, 11, 19, 21 (left), 23, 25; Newscom: Everett Collection, 27; Shutterstock: Julia Khimich (background), cover (right) and throughout, Nadegda Rozova (background), cover (left) and throughout; Superstock: Buyenlarge, 6

Direct Quotations
p. 8, from *Unforgivable Blackness: The Rise and Fall of Jack Johnson*, by Geoffrey C. Ward. New York: A. A. Knopf, 2004.
p. 29, from Oct. 8, 2020, *Talk Sport* article, "Jack Johnson Became the First Black Heavyweight Champion of the World, Inspiring Ali, Tyson and Hopkins by Literally Fighting Against Racism," talksport.com

Any additional websites and resources referenced in this book are not maintained, authorized, or sponsored by Capstone. All product and company names are trademarks™ or registered® trademarks of their respective holders.

TABLE OF CONTENTS

INTRODUCTION
The Fight of the Century................... 4

CHAPTER ONE
The Gloves Go On 8

CHAPTER TWO
Packing a Punch........................ 14

CHAPTER THREE
World Famous........................... 18

CHAPTER FOUR
Controversy............................ 22

CHAPTER FIVE
A Champion's Legacy.................... 26

    Glossary 30
    Read More 31
    Internet Sites 31
    Index............................... 32
    About the Author 32

Words in **bold** are in the glossary.

INTRODUCTION

THE FIGHT OF THE CENTURY

July 4, 1910, was a day that boxing fans had waited years to see. It was also a day that many dreaded. The fight between Jack Johnson, who was Black, and Jim Jeffries, who was white, was viewed as a battle for racial **superiority**.

By 1910, Jack Johnson was the best fighter in the world. He was also a loud, proud Black man. And he enjoyed the money and fame he had earned. This upset many white people. They searched for a "great white hope." They wanted someone to reclaim the honor of the white race by beating Johnson. They found former champion James J. Jeffries.

Jeffries came out of retirement to face Johnson. The 35-year-old was the **favorite** despite the clear physical advantage 32-year-old Johnson had.

On the day of the fight, about 12,000 people packed an arena in Reno, Nevada. Almost everybody was rooting for Jeffries.

But Johnson was in control of the fight from the opening bell. He later said he knew he had Jeffries beat after the fourth round. But the fight lasted 15 rounds. It ended when Jeffries's corner stopped the fight. Jeffries had already been knocked down three times.

Johnson knocking Jeffries down during their 1910 fight

But Johnson's victory had consequences. Race riots broke out across the country. Dozens were hurt. About 20 people were killed.

Johnson's win made two things clear. Johnson was a skilled boxer. And being Black, talented, and famous in the United States was both a blessing and a curse.

Johnson's life was filled with challenges and controversies. And his career would affect many boxing greats who came after him, like Muhammad Ali. This is Johnson's story.

The Johnson and Jeffries Fight Hits the Movie Theaters

The fight was filmed and shown in movie theaters. It broke box office records. In 1912, the United States Congress banned showings of all boxing title matches. They wanted to stop showings of the Johnson and Jeffries fight. They feared it would lead to racial violence.

CHAPTER ONE

THE GLOVES GO ON

Jack Johnson came from humble roots. He was born Arthur John Johnson on March 31, 1878, in Galveston, Texas, to Henry and Tina Johnson. His parents had been enslaved before the Civil War and worked low-paying jobs. He was the third of nine children.

Growing up in Galveston helped shape Johnson's views on race. The city was **segregated**. But relationships between Black and white people were surprisingly good.

Johnson had a mixed group of friends. "As I grew up, the white boys were my friends," he said. "I ate with them, played with them and slept at their homes. . . . No one ever taught me that white men were superior to me."

Johnson kept that attitude throughout his life. But he rarely found white people who agreed.

Galveston, Texas, in the late 1800s

For poor families like Johnson's family, working was a priority. After Johnson finished fifth grade, he dropped out of school to get a job. He started working odd jobs, including at the docks.

When Johnson was a teenager, he moved to Dallas. He worked with horses at a racetrack. While there, Johnson met Walter Lewis, the owner of a painting shop. Lewis was also interested in boxing. He encouraged Johnson to take up the sport. Johnson credited Lewis with teaching him how to box.

At 16 years old, Johnson moved to New York City. After leaving New York City, he lived and trained with a boxer named Barbados Joe Walcott in Boston.

Barbados Joe Walcott in the late 1800s

The next year, Johnson returned to Texas. He found a job at a gym owned by German fighter Herman Bernau. By this time, it was clear that the young man wanted to become a boxer.

But boxing was illegal in Texas. Johnson took part in battles royal at private clubs. These were **unlicensed** fights in which as many as eight Black fighters were put into a ring. They were told to box until there was only one man left standing.

In 1898, the 20-year-old Johnson landed his first professional fight. It was a match against Charley Brooks. He knocked out Brooks in the second round. It was the start of something big.

> **FACT** By the time Johnson started boxing, the sport had just become more organized. The first gloved heavyweight fight was in 1892. Before that, boxers did not wear gloves, they threw fewer punches, and there was more wrestling involved during matches.

Johnson around 1900

CHAPTER TWO

PACKING A PUNCH

Johnson began to make a name for himself in the boxing world. But he was still learning the sport. He primarily used his size and strength to overpower opponents. He wasn't skilled at some of the finer points of the sport, like defense and strategy.

Perhaps the biggest turning point in Johnson's career came during a defeat in 1901. That year, Johnson was back in Galveston. In a fight against veteran boxer Joe Choynski, Johnson met his match. He lost the contest. To add to the loss, both fighters were jailed for violating Texas's boxing ban.

While they were jailed together, something unexpected happened. Choynski recognized Johnson's **potential**. But he also knew the fighter's flaws. Choynski taught Johnson the art of defensive boxing—how to use his gloves to block punches and shift his body to deflect the force of punches.

Now, Johnson had power and skill.

Choynski and Johnson boxing in 1909

FACT Johnson and Choynski were jailed for 23 days for the illegal fight. But while in jail, the sheriff actually allowed people to come watch them box.

Johnson became a new fighter—with a new nickname. The "Galveston Giant" was on the rise. He moved out of Texas and up in the rankings. In 1902, he scored a major victory over Frank Childs, a former Black heavyweight champion. He followed that up by claiming his first title as the Black heavyweight champion in 1903. He beat "Denver" Ed Martin in a 20-round **decision**.

Johnson was the Black champion—but he wanted more. Many white boxers avoided fighting him. They did not want to lose to a Black boxer.

Finally, in 1908, Johnson defeated Tommy Burns—a white boxer—to win the heavyweight championship. The "Galveston Giant" was on top of the world.

Burns and Johnson's 1908 fight

CHAPTER THREE

WORLD FAMOUS

When Johnson captured the heavyweight champion title, his fame skyrocketed. Newspapers wrote about him. And he became the most photographed Black man of his time. Johnson enjoyed the spotlight. But that earned him many critics.

Johnson also traveled around the world. He saw places very few Black men could in the early twentieth century. From Australia to France, he was a celebrity everywhere he went.

In the ring, Johnson fought off most of his challengers, including the 1910 "Fight of the Century" against Jeffries. **Promoters** searched for a white boxer who could defeat Johnson but failed. And Johnson mostly refused to fight Black boxers. He could make more money fighting white opponents.

A crowd waits to see Johnson in New York City in 1910

Johnson became very wealthy, and he spent his money wildly. He invested in nightclubs in Chicago and New York. He also fell in love with the newest American invention—the automobile. Johnson bought dozens of cars and loved driving fast.

FACT Johnson enjoyed tinkering and received several patents for his creations. On April 18, 1922, Johnson patented his design for a wrench.

W.E.B. Du Bois   Booker T. Washington

While many Black people enjoyed seeing Johnson's **extravagant** life, others were disappointed. Black leaders like W.E.B. Du Bois and Booker T. Washington spoke out against Johnson. They believed his actions harmed the Black community because he did not use his fame to uplift the race.

Johnson didn't change. But his personal and professional life would soon be affected by racism.

CHAPTER FOUR

CONTROVERSY

Johnson marched to the beat of his own drum. This included his personal life. The boxer had relationships with several white women. During the early 1900s, this was practically unheard-of in the United States. There were many social and legal consequences. In a lot of places, interracial relationships were illegal. But Johnson didn't care.

In 1911, Johnson married Etta Duryea, a white New York **socialite**. Their relationship was rocky from the start. And Duryea suffered from depression. She died a year later. Johnson quickly remarried, this time to Lucille Cameron, another white woman.

In 1910, the government passed the Mann Act. This law prevented transporting women for "**immoral**" purposes. The government had its eyes on Johnson, whose relationships with white women were socially unacceptable. They used the Mann Act to punish him.

Johnson and Cameron around 1921

In 1912, Johnson was arrested and charged with violating the Mann Act because of his relationship with Cameron. She refused to testify, so there was no case.

The next year, the government brought another case against Johnson. This time, one of Johnson's former girlfriends cooperated. Johnson was sentenced to 366 days in prison.

Racism was at the heart of both cases. The government was eager to bring down a powerful, popular Black man.

While out on bail, Johnson and Cameron fled to France. He lived there for seven years. As a **fugitive**, Johnson became less marketable as a boxer. Promoters found it difficult to get crowds excited about seeing him fight. The time away also dulled his skills.

In 1915, Johnson fought white boxer Jess Willard in Cuba. He lost in the 26th round. Johnson was champion no more.

Willard knocks Johnson down in their 1915 fight.

CHAPTER FIVE

A CHAMPION'S LEGACY

In 1920, Johnson surrendered to U.S. officials and served his jail sentence. He wanted to come home.

Johnson continued fighting after his release but was never again a real contender. Having spent most of his money, Johnson took on various odd jobs and exhibition fights.

In 1924, he married for the third time, to a woman named Irene Pineau. They would remain married until his death.

On June 9, 1946, a segregated diner in North Carolina refused to serve Johnson and a friend. Johnson angrily sped away in his car. He crashed into a pole and later died from his injuries. He was 68 years old.

Johnson and Pineau in France in 1933

Over the years, Johnson's legacy has grown. His story was the basis of the 1967 play *The Great White Hope*, which was also made into a film. He was inducted into the Boxing Hall of Fame in 1990. And in 2004, the Ken Burns documentary on Johnson's life, *Unforgivable Blackness*, aired on the Public Broadcasting Service.

It would take until 2018 for the biggest wrong against Johnson to be corrected. After years of attempts, the boxer was granted a presidential **pardon** for his 1913 conviction under the Mann Act. The government finally acknowledged that Johnson's conviction was racially motivated.

A skilled and willful Black man at a time when it was costly to be both, Johnson was an imperfect but important example of living life on one's own terms.

Johnson in 1931

Ali: Another Bold Champion

After Jack Johnson, there were several great Black heavyweight champions, including Joe Louis. But no one compared to Muhammad Ali. Like Johnson, he didn't let anyone tell him what he could or could not do. And Ali too angered white people with his boastful nature and dominance in the ring.

Ali's religious beliefs and Black pride would land him on government watch lists and eventually get him convicted of a crime. Ali refused to fight in the Vietnam War when drafted. Ali did not flee. Instead, he suffered through an exile from boxing that robbed the champion of some of his best years.

Ali always spoke highly of Johnson in interviews, acknowledging the difficult times in which the former champion lived. "Jack Johnson was a big inspiration because of what he did outside of the ring. He was so bold," Ali once said.

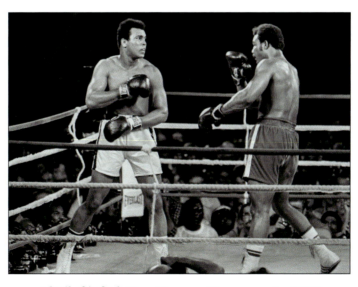

Ali (left) fighting George Foreman in 1974

GLOSSARY

decision (di-SIZH-uhn)—the final score of a fight

extravagant (ik-STRAV-uh-guhnt)—going beyond what is reasonable or expected

favorite (FAY-vruht)—the person or team predicted to win a sporting event

fugitive (FYOO-juh-tiv)—a person charged with a crime who runs away from the law

immoral (ih-MOR-uhl)—considered bad or wrong

pardon (PAHR-duhn)—an act of official forgiveness for a serious offense

potential (puh-TEN-chuhl)—ability that could be developed

promoter (pruh-MOH-tur)—a person or company that puts on a sporting event

segregated (SEG-ruh-gay-ted)—separated by race

socialite (SOH-shuh-lahyt)—a person who is popular in society

superiority (suh-peer-ee-OR-ih-tee)—being better than someone or something else

unlicensed (un-LYE-suhnst)—done without permission

READ MORE

Fishman, Jon M. *Boxing's G.O.A.T.: Muhammad Ali, Manny Pacquiao, and More.* Minneapolis: Lerner, 2022.

Patterson, James and Kwame Alexander. *Becoming Muhammad Ali.* New York: Jimmy Patterson Books, 2020.

Tyner, Artika R. *The Untold Story of A. Philip Randolph: Union Organizer and Civil Rights Activist.* North Mankato, MN: Capstone, 2025.

INTERNET SITES

Britannica Kids: Jack Johnson
kids.britannica.com/students/article/Jack-Johnson/275167

Kiddle: Jack Johnson (Boxer) Facts for Kids
kids.kiddle.co/Jack_Johnson_(boxer)

Public Broadcasting Service: About Jack Johnson
pbs.org/kenburns/unforgivable-blackness/about-johnson

INDEX

Ali, Muhammad, 7, 29
Australia, 18

Bernau, Herman, 12
Boston, Massachusetts, 10
Boxing Hall of Fame, 28
Brooks, Charley, 12
Burns, Tommy, 16, 17

Cameron, Lucille, 22, 23, 24
Chicago, 20
Childs, Frank, 16
Choynski, Joe, 14, 15
Cuba, 25

Dallas, Texas, 10
Du Bois, W.E.B., 21
Duryea, Etta, 22

Foreman, George, 29
France, 18, 24, 27

Galveston, Texas, 8, 9, 14
Great White Hope, The, 28

Jeffries, James J., 4–7, 18
Johnson, Henry, 8
Johnson, Tina, 8

Lewis, Walter, 10
Louis, Joe, 29

Mann Act, 22, 24, 28
Martin, "Denver" Ed, 16

New York City, 10, 19, 20, 22
North Carolina, 26

Pineau, Irene, 26, 27

racial superiority, 4
Reno, Nevada, 6

Unforgivable Blackness, 28
United States Congress, 7

Walcott, Barbados Joe, 10, 11
Washington, Booker T., 21
Willard, Jess, 25

ABOUT THE AUTHOR

Elliott Smith is a freelance writer, editor, and author. He has covered a wide variety of subjects, including sports, entertainment, and travel, for newspapers, magazines, and websites. He has written a nonfiction book about the Washington Nationals and a children's book about Bryce Harper. He lives in the Washington, DC, area with his wife and two children.